MARS
Explorer

TJ Rob

MARS Explorer
By TJ Rob

Copyright Text TJ Rob, 2017
All rights reserved. No part of the book may be reproduced in any form without permission in writing from the author. Reviewers may quote brief passages in review.

Disclaimer
No part of this book may be reproduced in any form or by any means, mechanical or electronic, including photocopying or recording, or by an information storage and retrieval system, or transmitted by email without permission in writing from the publisher. This book is for entertainment purposes only. The views expressed are those of author alone.

Published by:
TJ Rob
Suite 609
440-10816 Macleod Trail SE
Calgary, AB T2J 5N8   www.TJRob.com

ISBN 978-1-988695-00-6

Photo Credits: Images used under license from Flickr.com, Public Domain, Wikimedia Commons: Cover page, Pixabay.com / Public Domain; Back Page, Pixabay.com / Public Domain; pg. 1, Holidayextras / Flickr.com; pg. 2, David Crisp and the WFPC2 Science Team (JPL/CalTech) / [Public Domain via Wikimedia Commons; pg. 3, David Crisp and the WFPC2 Science Team (JPL/CalTech) / [Public Domain via Wikimedia Commons; pg. 4, WP CC BY-SA 3.0 / Wikimedia Commons; pg. 5, WP CC BY-SA 3.0 / Wikimedia Commons; pg. 6, Kevin Gill / Flickr.com; pg. 7, Nasa / Public Domain; pg. 8, Jean-Pol GRANDMONT CC BY 3.0 / Wikimedia Commons; pg. 9, Kevin Gill / Flickr.com; pg. 10, Inspiration Mars Foundation CC BY-SA 2.0 / Wikimedia Commons; pg. 11, Public Domain; pg. 12, NASA / Public Domain; pg. 13, NASA / Public Domain; pg. 15, NASA / Public Domain; pg. 16, NASA / Public Domain via Wikimedia Commons; pg. 17, NASA / Public Domain via Wikimedia Commons; pg. 18, NASA Bill Stafford / Public Domain via Wikimedia Commons ; pg. 19, NASA / Public Domain; pg. 20, NASA/JPL/Corby Waste / Public Domain via Wikimedia Commons; pg. 21, NASA / Public Domain; pg. 22, NASA/JPL/Corby Waste / Public Domain via Wikimedia Commons; pg. 23, NASA/JPL-Caltech/Malin Space Science Systems / Public Domain; pg. 24, NASA/ Goddard Space Flight Center / Wikimedia Commons; pg. 25, Nesnad CC BY-SA 4.0-3.0-2.5-2.0-1.0 /], via Wikimedia Commons; pg. 26, NASA/JPL-Caltech/Malin Science Space Systems / Public Domain; pg. 27, NASA/JPL-Caltech/Malin Science Space Systems / Public Domain; pg. 28, David Crisp and the WFPC2 Science Team (JPL/CalTech) / [Public Domain via Wikimedia Commons; pg. 28, NASA / Public Domain; pg. 29, David Crisp and the WFPC2 Science Team (JPL/CalTech) / [Public Domain via Wikimedia Commons; pg. 29, NASA / Public Domain; pg. 29, Public Domain; pg. 30, David Crisp and the WFPC2 Science Team (JPL/CalTECH) / [Public Domain via Wikimedia Commons; pg. 30, NASA / Public Domain; pg. 30, Public Domain; pg. 31, NASA / Public Domain; pg. 32, NASA/JPL / Public Domain; pg. 33, NASA/JPL-Caltech / Public Domain; pg. 34, Sémhur / Wikimedia Commons; pg. 35, NASA/Corbis / Public Domain via Wikimedia Commons; pg. 36, Kevin Gill / Flickr.com; pg. 37, NASA/USGS / Public Domain; pg. 38, NASA Ames Research Center - NASA Ames featured images / Public Domain; pg. 39, NASA / Public Domain

TABLE OF CONTENTS

	Page
Where is Mars?	4
Mars— A Mystery?	6
Who or What is Mars named after?	8
How far away is Mars?	9
Why do we want to explore other planets?	10
Why Mars and not Venus?	11
What makes Mars the best planet to explore?	12
How long is the journey to Mars?	13
How could we get to Mars?	14
Living in Space	18
Previous Missions to Mars (2001 — 2004)	20
Previous Missions to Mars (2005 — 2012)	22
Previous Missions to Mars (2013 — 2014)	24
What did they find on Mars?	26
Mars VS Earth — Differences?	28
Communicating with Mars	32
7 Interesting Mars Facts	33
Amazing features on Mars — Mons Olympus	34
Amazing features on Mars — Valles Marineris	36
A Future Colony on Mars?	38
Please leave a review and Other EXCITING books by TJ Rob	40

Where is Mars?

Mercury Venus Earth **Mars**

Jupiter   Saturn   Uranus   Neptune

Mars is :

— the fourth planet from the sun in the Solar System.

— the next planet beyond Earth.

— the planet between Earth and the giant planet Jupiter.

— the second smallest planet in the Solar System.

Mars — A Mystery?

Mars has been a mystery to humans for thousands of years. We could see the planet, but details of Mars' surface are difficult to see from Earth.

Using telescopes from Earth we were able see features on Mars that changed with the seasons. We also could observe white patches at the very top and very bottom of the planet (the poles of Mars).

For many years people thought that bright and dark areas on Mars were patches of vegetation.

In 1965 the Mariner 4 spacecraft flew by Mars taking photos of the surface. These photos show that Mars has a desert-like surface covered in craters.

Mars seemed to be a dead planet.

Later missions showed that Mars is a complex planet and holds many mysteries yet to be solved.

Who or what is Mars named after?

The Ancient Romans named the planet after the Roman god of war called Mars.

Both the ancient Romans and the ancient Greeks associated the planet with war because its color resembles the color of blood.

Other civilizations also gave the planet names based on its color — for example, the Egyptians named it "Her Desher " meaning "the red one".

The ancient Chinese astronomers called Mars "the fire star".

Mars is often called the Red planet. Rock and dust covering its surface is rich in iron, giving it it's red color.

How far away is Mars?

To determine how long it will take to reach Mars, we must first know the distance between the Earth and Mars.

The distance between the two planets is constantly changing as they travel around the sun.

The closest that Earth and Mars are to each other is when Mars is at its closest point to the sun and Earth is at its farthest from the Sun.

The closest the two planets have been in human history was in 2003, when they were only 34.8 million miles (56 million km) apart.

At their farthest point from each other, Earth and Mars are 250 million miles (401 million km) apart.

Why do we want to explore other planets?

Humans are curious.

We want to find out what is out there in space. We want to know what life is like on other planets.

Is there life on other planets in the Solar System that is similar to our own planet? Or are they different from Earth?

Could we live on other planets, like Mars? Could Mars become another home for humans in the far future?

These are the reasons that we explore space.

Mars is our first stop in the exploration for life on other planets.

Why Mars and not Venus?

Venus is a lot closer to Earth than Mars is. At its closest point to Earth, Venus is only 25 million miles (40 million km) away. When Mars is closest to Earth, it is 34 million miles (55 million km) away. The shorter distance of Earth to Venus means you would need less time and fuel to get there, reducing the cost.

Venus is lot less friendly than Mars.

We can't land on the surface of Venus. The average temperature is over 900 degrees, enough to melt metal. The pressure from the weight of the air on the surface of Venus is so powerful that it would crush you like a bug. It is 90 times more powerful than on the weight of the air on the surface on Earth.

It would be almost impossibly difficult to design a spacecraft that could survive Venus's hellish environment.

To make it worse, Venus has rain made of Sulphuric Acid.

Nights on Venus last for 120 Earth days.

Humans cannot live on Mars without the help of technology, but compared to Venus it's paradise! Venus would not be a good choice!

What makes Mars the best planet to explore?

Mars is close enough to Earth. All the other planets are either too far away or not friendly enough for humans to live on. After Earth, Mars is the most habitable planet in our Solar System for these reasons:

1. Its soil contains some water to grow food and for drinking
2. It isn't too cold or too hot
3. There is enough sunlight to use solar panels to make energy
4. Gravity on Mars is 38% that of our Earth's, which humans may be able to adapt to
5. It has a thin atmosphere that offers some protection from radiation
6. A Mars day is 24 hours, 39 minutes and 35 seconds — not so different from Earth

How long is the journey to Mars?

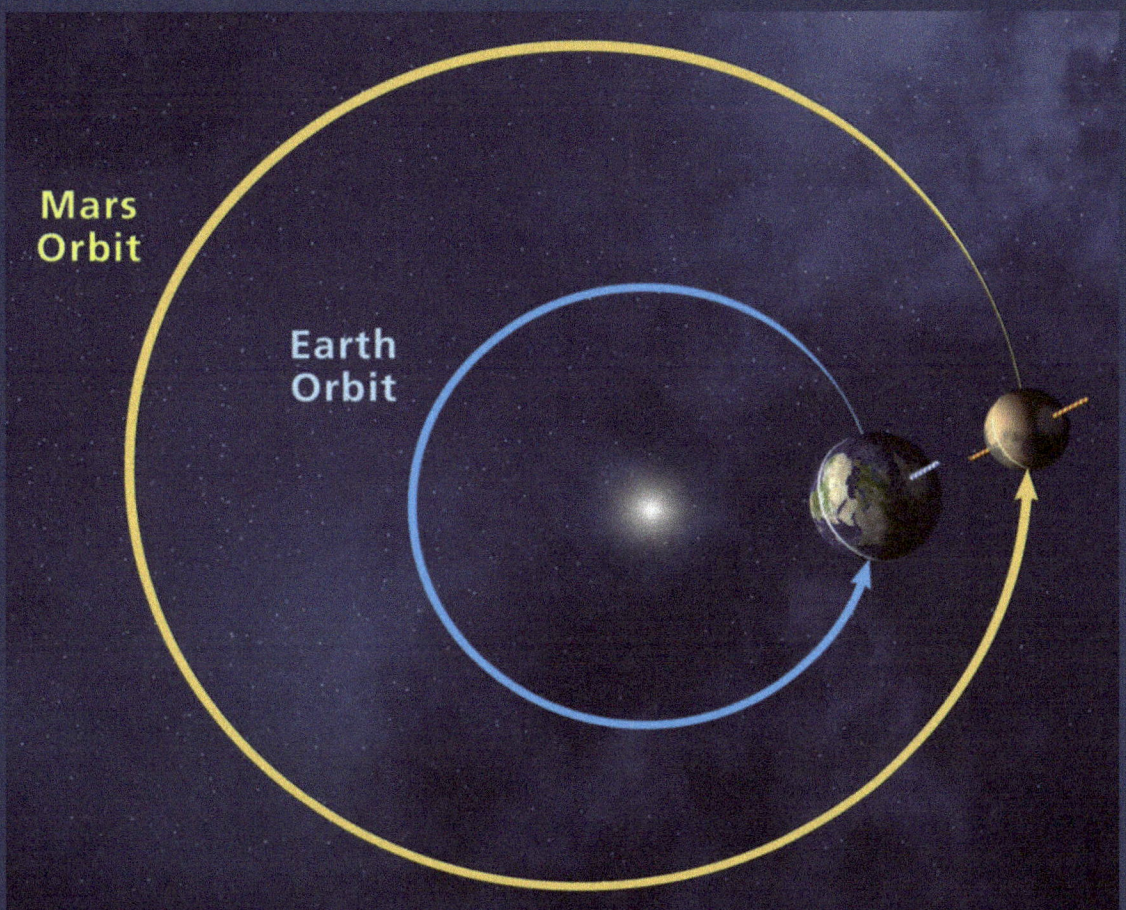

Mars and Earth are both orbiting the Sun, which means that when a spacecraft is launched from Earth it has to be aimed at where Mars is going to be, not where Mars is at the time of the launch.

To get to Mars from Earth could take between 150 and 300 days. This depends on 3 things —

1. How close Mars is to Earth
2. How fast the spacecraft can travel
3. The exact travel path that the spacecraft will take

The other problem is fuel. More fuel can allow the spacecraft to travel faster - but more fuel is also heavier. The spacecraft needs to make sure it carries enough fuel to get to Mars and back to Earth, but not so much that it makes the spacecraft too heavy to fly.

How could we get to Mars?

NASA (the National Aeronautics and Space Administration) of the USA is developing a huge rocket called the Space Launch System, or SLS.

This rocket is a heavy-lift launch vehicle. The SLS will enable astronauts to explore destinations far into the Solar System.

The SLS is the most powerful rocket ever built, capable of taking human explorers into space.

It will fly farther than any spacecraft built for humans has ever flown.

The SLS has 10 to 20 percent more power than the Saturn V rockets used to launch the Apollo moon missions in the late 1960s and early 1970s.

It will be able to carry more cargo into space than any spacecraft before - up to 130 tons or 260,000 pounds (118,000 kg).

The SLS will be taller than a 32 story building, standing at over 322 feet (98 m) high off the ground.

The SLS is also one of the most expensive rockets ever built — the estimated costs are close to $18 Billion.

Unmanned test flights of the SLS with no astronauts on board are planned for 2018. The first expected manned flights with astronauts is planned for 2021.

Orion

Orion ("o-rie-un") is a new NASA spacecraft for astronauts.

What Will Orion Do?

Orion will carry astronauts into deep space and then return them home to Earth. The SLS rocket will carry Orion beyond low Earth orbit.

After reaching low Earth orbit, Orion will break away from the SLS and continue onto its final destination — Mars or even farther into the Solar System

Orion

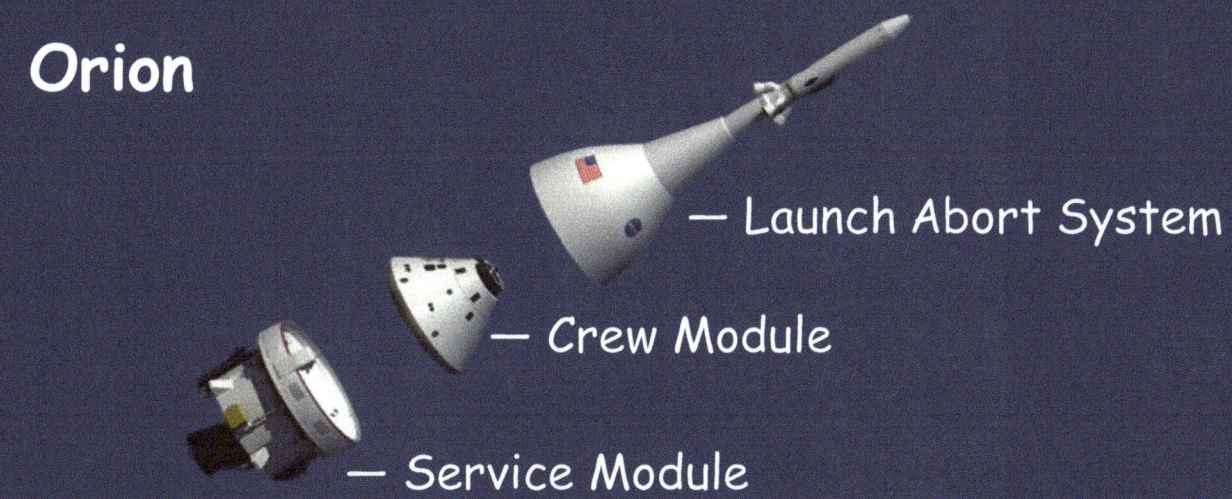

— Launch Abort System
— Crew Module
— Service Module

Orion has three main parts. The upper section is the Launch Abort System, or LAS; the Crew Module is the middle part; and the Service Module is the lower portion of the spacecraft.

If an emergency occurs during launch or the climb to orbit, the LAS would activate in milliseconds. It would propel the Crew Module away from the rocket to safety. The LAS looks like a tower on top of the crew module.

Astronauts will sit in the middle section, the Crew Module. This will be their living quarters.

Beneath the crew module is the Service Module. It holds the power and propulsion systems. Solar array panels on the Service Module will absorb sunlight to create electricity. This power will allow the spacecraft to remain in orbit for months at a time.

Orion will carry up to six astronauts.

Living in Space

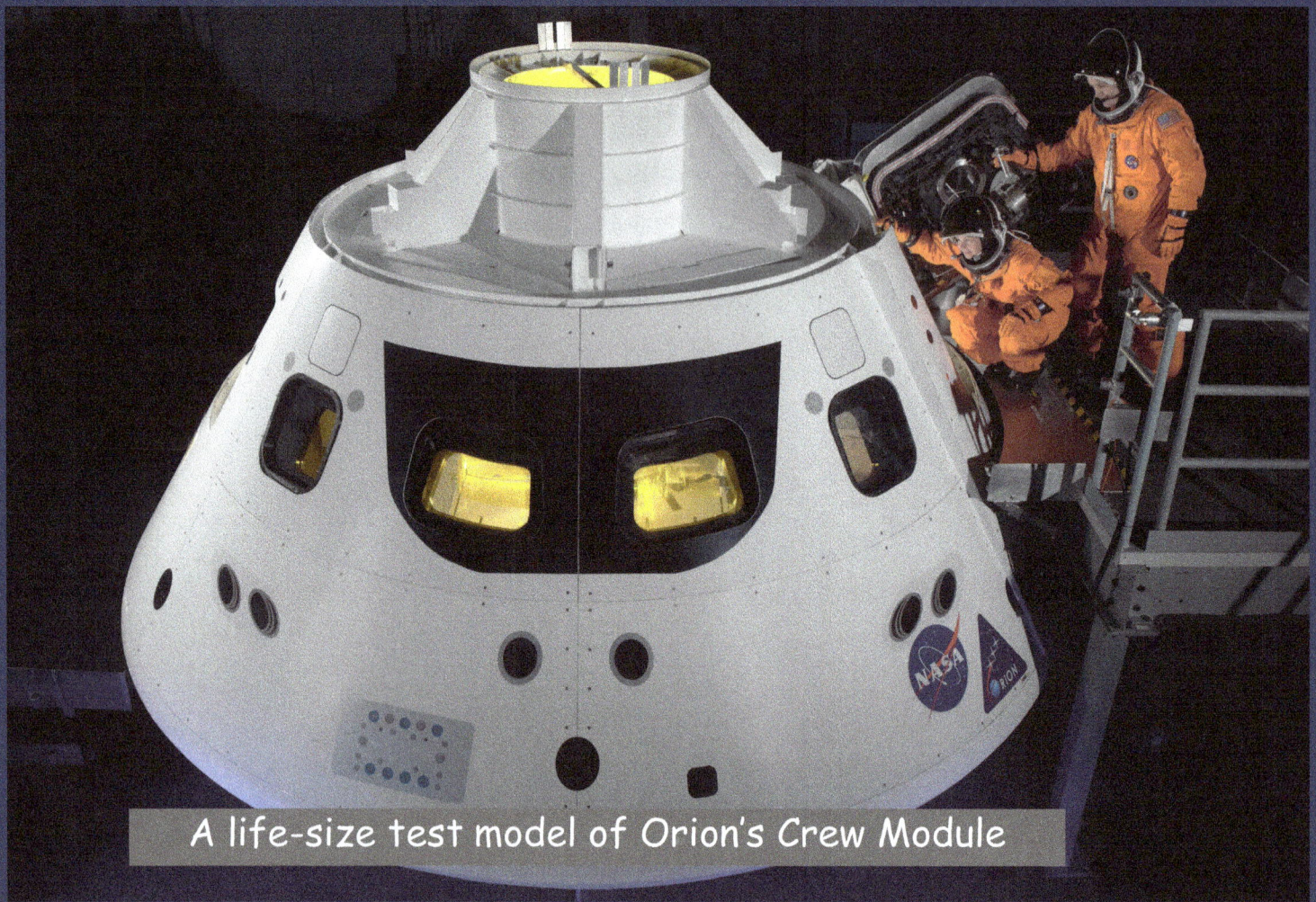

A life-size test model of Orion's Crew Module

A spacecraft like Orion will be pretty small inside. The estimates for Orion's size is about 16 to 17 feet (5 m) across (diameter) - which is about the same as the length of a medium sized SUV vehicle.

When astronauts in the Orion spacecraft travel beyond the moon to explore deep space destinations, they will need good food to keep them healthy. There are challenges feeding the crew on deep space missions.

Orion has limited room inside it to keep all the supplies and food astronauts will need during their missions. A journey to Mars and back to Earth could take more than 2 years. The Orion crew will have to take everything they need with them. That's a lot of food and other equipment to keep in a very small spacecraft.

The more they take with them the heavier the spacecraft that is needed. A heavier spacecraft needs more fuel and energy to get it to its destination, and there are no gas stations along the way to get more fuel.

To help cut down on the amount of supplies Orion will carry for its crew, scientists are developing a variety of food bars that astronauts can eat for breakfast during their spaceflight missions. Scientists have to consider how the bars will affect crew morale. Having a choice of different foods, as well as good tasting ones is important. We all know how eating the same food can become very boring.

Breakfast food bars for astronauts

Scientists are also working to grow and produce food in space for very long missions.

The International Space Station is doing tests on how to grow fresh vegetables in space.

Scientists are also looking at how to package food items to keep them fresh even in places where there are huge temperature differences, such as the surface of Mars. The surface of Mars can be extremely cold at night and extremely hot during the day.

Previous Missions to Mars

Since the 1960s there have been over 40 unmanned missions to Mars. Only 18 were successful. The rest were destroyed on launch or lost in space or when they landed on the planet. Some unmanned mission spacecraft landed on the planet but were damaged, so we could not communicate with them from Earth.

Over the last 15 years space agencies have had more successful missions. NASA's Mars Odyssey in 2001 and the European Space Agency's Mars Express in 2003 were successful launches. Both spacecraft are still currently operating in Mars orbit.

2001 Mars Odyssey

2003 Mars Express

In 2004 the 2 Mars Exploration Rovers Spirit and Opportunity settled onto the Martian surface. They began searching for evidence of water on the planet. Spirit lasted for about 7 years and Opportunity is still operating.

The images and data from both Spirit and Opportunity have helped scientists understand about the surface of Mars and the existence of water there in the distant past. Their images and data have given scientists valuable long-term daily looks at the weather and climate of the planet, as well.

2004   Mars Rovers Opportunity and Spirit

Previous Missions to Mars

The Mars Reconnaissance Orbiter launched in 2005 has continually mapped and imaged the planet at high resolution since then. It provides a useful radio link back to Earth.

In 2008 Mars Phoenix landed on the Red Planet and spent several months cataloguing conditions near the Mars Northern Polar regions.

2005   Mars Reconnaissance Oribiter

2008   Mars Phoenix landing on Mars

In 2012 a new, bigger Rover called Curiosity was sent to Mars and is making important discoveries right now.

2012 — Mars Rover Curiosity

Previous Missions to Mars

The two most recent missions to arrive at Mars are the MAVEN mission (2013) and the Indian Space Research Organization's Mars Orbiter Mission (nicknamed "MOM") in 2014.

MAVEN is an atmospheric studies satellite that is sampling the upper atmosphere to understand how the planet is losing its atmosphere (and how it may have lost water in the past).

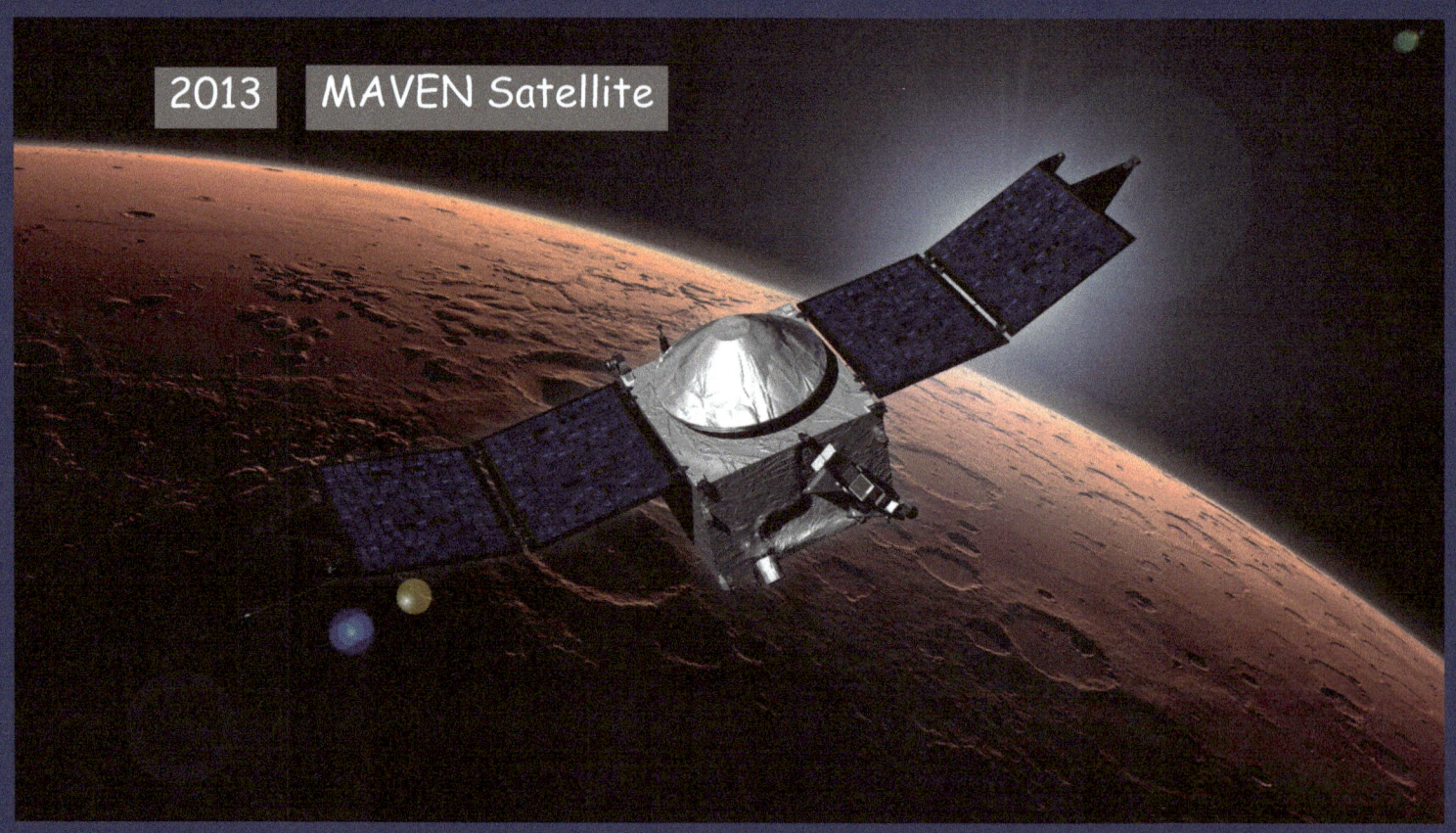

2013 MAVEN Satellite

The MOM mission has been returning images of the planet and data about the atmosphere.

2014 MOM Orbiter

What did they find on Mars?

The 3 Rovers and the other unmanned missions to Mars have uncovered some interesting facts about the planet.

Water:

There was no water on the surface that the Rovers have found, but water has been found in a layer under the surface.

Water ice was found in an underground layer in a large region of Mars about halfway from the equator to the North Pole.

The amount of water in this deposit is about as much as in Lake Superior. It was found using radar aboard a spacecraft orbiting Mars.

This water could be used by future astronauts.

Air:

There is no breathable air on Mars.

Chemicals and Minerals:

The Rover Curiosity was able to drill into rocks on the Martian surface and found a whole bunch of minerals and chemicals that would be necessary for life to exist. They found sulfur, nitrogen, hydrogen, oxygen, phosphorus and carbon. The fine-grained rock also contains clay minerals, suggesting a long-ago water environment — perhaps a lake.

Soil Conditions:

There is no soil on which to grow food on Mars — only rock dust. For plants to grow there needs to be microbes in the soil to give plants the nutrients that they need. So far no microbes have been found.

Radiation

The Curiosity Rover detected dangerous levels of radiation. Unlike Earth, Mars has a very thin atmosphere that does not give enough protection to humans from radiation from the Sun and from cosmic rays from Space.

Curiosity detected radiation levels that were higher than expected and would cause serious damage to astronauts. Now that we know what the actual levels of radiation on Mars are, engineers can build spacecraft and spacesuits that are able to protect humans on deep space missions.

Mars vs Earth — Differences?

SIZE:

Earth
7926 Miles
12756 Km

Mars 1/2
4220 Miles
6792 Km

Earth's Moon 1/4
2159 Miles
3475 Km

MASS:

Earth

Mars

Earth has 10 times the mass of Mars. Earth weighs 10 times more than Mars

GRAVITY:

Mars has only 38% of the gravity on Earth.

On Mars

On Earth

The same jump is 2.63 times higher on Mars than on Earth!

Earth 10 foot (3m) dunk.　　　　Mars 26.3 foot (8 m) dunk.

Mars vs Earth — Differences?

WEIGHT:

You weigh a lot less on Mars!

If you weigh 100 pounds on Earth, you would only weigh 38 pounds on Mars.

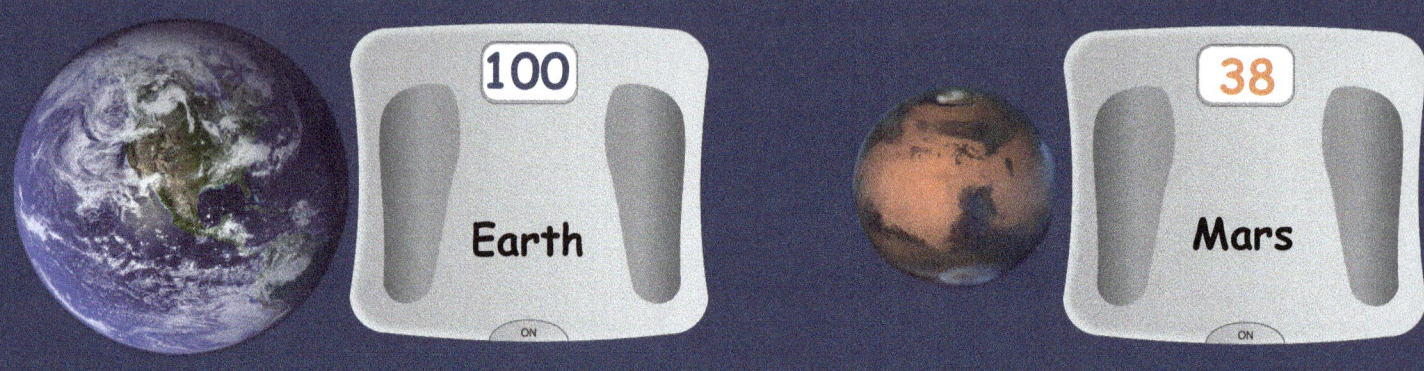

TIME:

Days and Years are longer on Mars than on Earth

	Earth	Mars
1 Day	24 Hours	24 Hours + 40 Minutes
1 Year	365 Earth Days	687 Earth Days

MOONS:

The Earth has only 1 large moon. Mars has two small moons.

Earth's Moon is over 150 times bigger than any of Mars' moons.

The 2 moons around Mars are Phobos and Deimos. They are named after the sons of Ares, the Greek god of war. Phobos means "fear," and Deimos means "flight."

Both Phobos and Deimos are shaped like potatoes. They have too little mass for gravity to make them spherical (round) like our moon.

Phobos

13.8 Miles (22.2 km)

Deimos

7.8 Miles (12.6 km)

Phobos is the larger of Mars' 2 moons. It orbits closer to the planet's surface and completes 3 orbits of Mars every day — about once every 7.5 hours.

Phobos is getting closer and closer to Mars at a rate of 6 feet (1.8 m) every 100 years. In about 50 million years time, Phobos will either crash into Mars or break up into a ring just like Saturn's rings.

Deimos is the smaller of Mars' two moons. Deimos orbits around Mars every 30 hours.

Communicating with Mars?

With the incredible distances between Earth and Mars, scientists have problems when they communicate with Mars.

When Earth and Mars are at their closest point of 33.9 million miles (54.6 million km) away, it would take a signal from Earth about 3 minutes to make the journey to Mars, and then another 3 minutes for the signals to get back to Earth.

When Earth and Mars are at their most distant point, it takes more than 21 minutes to send a signal to Mars, and then another 21 minutes to receive a return message.

7 Interesting Mars Facts

1. Mars has the largest dust storms in the Solar System. They can last for months and cover the entire planet. These dust storms can have wind speeds of 125 miles per hour (201 km/h) and can reach as high as 30 miles (50 km) above the planet's surface.

2. Mars has 4 Seasons, just like planet Earth. Mars also has Winter, Spring, Summer and Fall. This is because of the similarity in the tilt of the rotation axis of both planets. The difference is that each season on Mars lasts twice as long as that on Earth.

3. Antarctica's deserts are the closest you can get to knowing what it would feel like to be on Mars. But even the most extreme conditions in Antarctica cannot equal the actual environment of the Red Planet. Unlike Mars, Antarctica is still able to sustain some forms of life.

4. Pieces of Mars have fallen to Earth. Scientists have found tiny traces of Martian atmosphere within meteorites which were violently ejected from Mars. They then orbited amongst galactic debris for millions of years before crash landing on Earth. These meteorites allowed scientists to begin studying Mars before launching space missions.

5. On Mars the Sun appears about half the size that it does on Earth.

6. Because Mars has almost no atmosphere, its sunrises and sunsets appear to be blue.

7. Mars' Northern and Southern hemispheres are so different they could be different planets. The Southern hemisphere is heavily cratered with a high elevation. The Northern hemisphere has a lower elevation with fewer craters. Scientists believe a meteor the size of Pluto once hit Mars creating the smoother Northern region of the planet.

Amazing Features on Mars

Olympus Mons

Mars has the largest volcano in the Solar System – Olympus Mons.

It measures 370 miles (600 km) across and rises nearly 16 miles (27 km) above the surrounding area. This volcano is 3 times higher than Mount Everest, Earth's highest mountain.

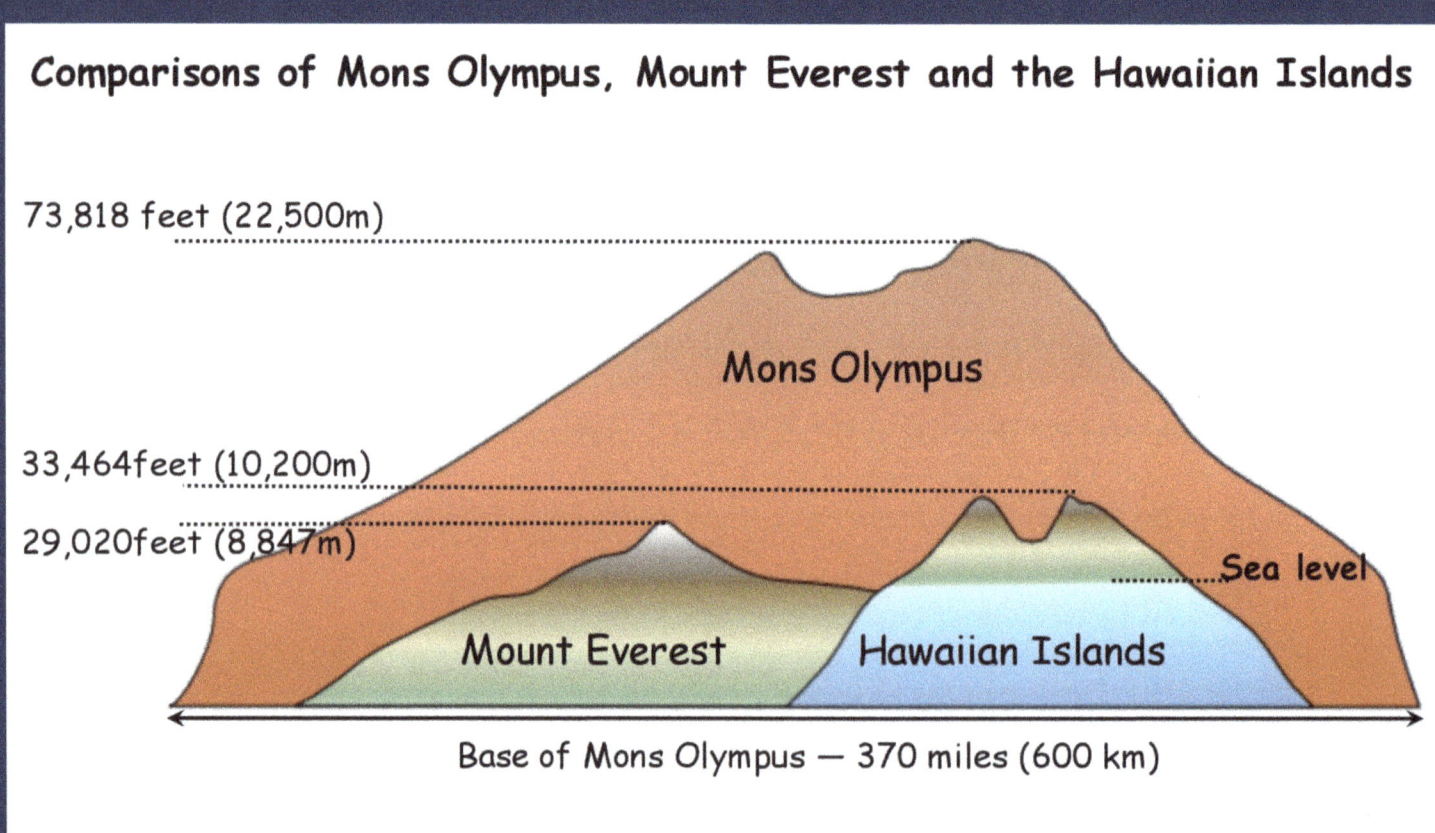

Mons Olympus

Mons Olympus is a shield volcano built by the continuous action of flowing lava over millions and millions of years that began some 3 billion years ago.

No volcanic eruptions have ever been recorded on Mars in real time. There is evidence of volcanic eruptions in the past, 20 to 30 million years ago. It is possible that Mars is not yet volcanically dead.

Amazing Features on Mars

Valles Marineris – Mariner Valleys

The Valles Marineris is an extensive canyon system on the Mars Equator. It is 2,500 miles (4,200 km) long and in places is 5 miles (7 km) deep. Valles Marineris is Latin for Mariner Valleys. It was named after the Mariner 9 Mars orbiter of 1971-72 which discovered it.

If you placed the Valles Marineris on Earth it would cross the USA. It is more than 10 times the length of the Grand Canyon. The Valles Marineris is also more than 4 times deeper than the Grand Canyon.

Valles Marineris

Valles Marineris

The Valles Marineris was formed about 3.5 billion years ago when 2 tectonic plates began splitting the surface.

At the same time, molten volcanic lava pushed the region up from below. In the valleys, the ground sank and underground water escaped. That caused the ground to drop farther and landslides and erosion continued to cut away and widen the valley systems.

Today, the Vallis Marineris shows the marks of ancient floods. The canyon continues to be eroded by the strong Martian winds.

A Future Colony on Mars?

Even with all the unmanned spacecraft and Rovers of the last 20 years, humans are still a long way from landing on Mars. It may still be another 20 years before we are able to land humans on Mars.

There are many challenges to conquer. How to survive the long journey to get there and how to survive the harsh environment once we land on the planet. And how to stay there for long periods of time.

Scientists and engineers are working hard to conquer all the challenges, and in the future we may set up a permanent human colony on Mars.

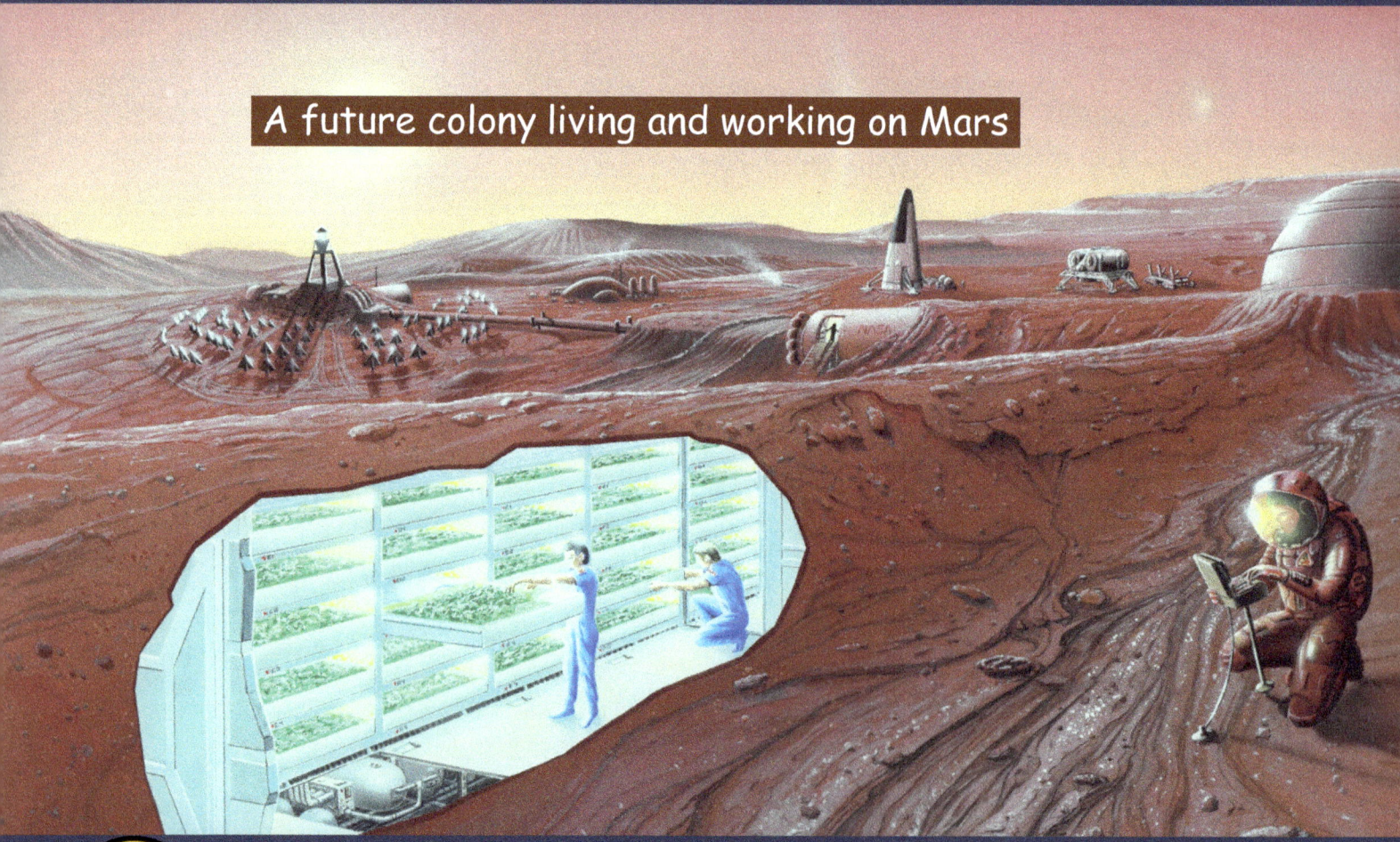

A future colony living and working on Mars

Growing food on the future Mars colony

Here are some of the challenges to setting up a colony on Mars:

— We will need to be able to shelter from the much colder Martian temperatures. The temperatures can drop to -195 degrees F (-125 C). A summer day on Mars may get up to 70 degrees F (20 C) near the Equator, but at night the temperature can plummet to about -100 degrees F (-73 C).

— Because Mars has such a thin atmosphere , we will need to be protected from the dangerous Solar and Space radiation.

— We will need to grow our own food and have a supply of water to survive. We will also need to make all the energy to power the colony.

— Because of the huge distances back to Earth, a colony on Mars will have to be fully self-contained. In an emergency it would take too long for any help to come from Earth.

THANKS FOR READING!

Please leave a review at the website where you bought this book and tell others what you liked about it.

Visit www.TJRob.com to get a FREE eBook and to learn about other exciting books by TJ Rob:

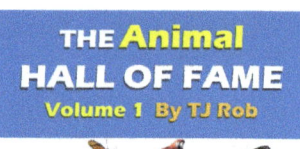

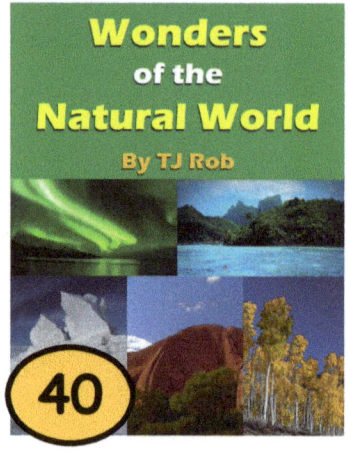
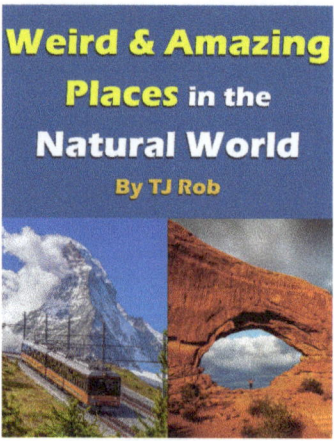
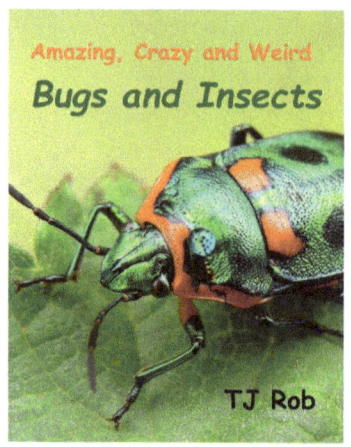
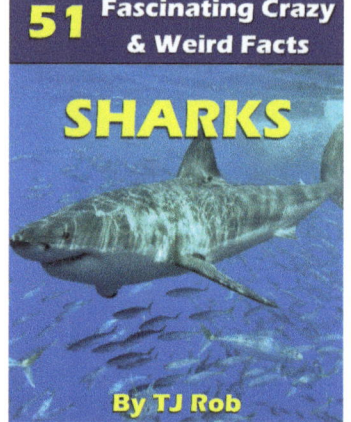

www.ingramcontent.com/pod-product-compliance
Lightning Source LLC
Chambersburg PA
CBHW040005080526
44586CB00027B/2885